NEVILLE
CHAMBERLAIN

A Life from Beginning to End

BY HOURLY HISTORY

Copyright © 2024 by Hourly History.

All rights reserved.

The cover photo is a derivative of "Right Honourable Neville Chamberlain" (https://commons.wikimedia.org/wiki/File:Right_Honourable_Neville_Chamberlain._Wellcome_M0003096.jpg) by Lafayette, used under CC BY 4.0 (https://creativecommons.org/licenses/by/4.0/deed.en)

Table of Contents

Introduction
Early Life
Chamberlain during World War I
In the Face of Economic and Political Instability
Becoming Prime Minister
The High Cost of Peace
The March to War
A False Peace and a Phoney War
Chamberlain Resigns
The Last Days of Neville Chamberlain
Conclusion
Bibliography

Introduction

Arthur Neville Chamberlain was born on March 18, 1869, in Birmingham, England, to Florence and Joseph Chamberlain. His father was a successful businessman and politician who held several government posts, including a term as mayor of Birmingham. Florence was Joseph's second wife; his first wife had died during the birth of their son, Austen. Five years after that tragedy, Joseph remarried Florence, and together they welcomed Neville along with three sisters—Ethel, Ida, and Hilda—into the world.

Neville's early childhood was a happy one, but everything changed when his mother died when he was just six years old. Her passing left a deep void in the Chamberlain household, and Joseph, overwhelmed by grief, never remarried and instead buried himself in work. The raising of his children, in the meantime, was left to Joseph's sisters. Neville's relationship with his surviving family members would later be described as respectful, perhaps even cordial, but never too warm and affectionate. It was apparently the kind of environment where everyone did what they could to stay on each other's good side, but they kept their distance, and no one got too close.

In many ways, these family dynamics could do much to explain Neville Chamberlain's later approach to politics on the world stage. Much of his later efforts to keep Britain (and the rest of the world) from being ensnared in World War II could be said to have been a high-wire balancing act of deference and distancing. He navigated a complex web of international tensions and tried to keep multiple parties content (one might even say appeased) while doing what he could to keep Britain from getting too close to the fray. But as Neville Chamberlain would learn later in life, this disengagement would come at a rather high price.

Chapter One

Early Life

"Partly the tradition of the family and partly my own incapacity to look on and see other people mismanage things drive me on to take up new and alas! unremunerative occupations."

—Neville Chamberlain

When Neville was growing up, his father was one of the most well-known figures in British public life, and his older half-brother, Austen, was carving out his own political career. It seemed like Neville was naturally set up for a life in politics too, being born into such a politically-minded family.

Yet that wasn't the plan his father had for him. From an early age, it was clear that Austen was the one groomed to take up the family's political legacy. His education and training were all aimed at preparing him for a life in public service. Austen went to the prestigious Trinity College, Cambridge, where he studied history and even became vice-president of the Union. After that, he traveled around Europe to gain experience in contemporary affairs before being elected to Parliament at age 29.

Neville, on the other hand, had a very different path laid out for him; he was to take over the business side of things. He was homeschooled until the age of 13. Then, in 1882, the young Neville Chamberlain began attending Rugby School, a boarding school some 35 miles (60 kilometers) from Birmingham. It might not sound like much to modern readers, but this was a top-notch institution for the time and place where Neville grew up. Most importantly for those seeking a higher station in life, the school had a reputation for being a fast track to success.

However, Chamberlain apparently had a hard go of the place since he was mercilessly teased by his peers. He would always be quiet and somewhat awkward in social situations, and as such, he didn't last long at the boarding school and was soon back home. It was then in 1886 that he tried his luck at Mason College (better known today as the University of Birmingham). Here, he took courses in engineering, science, and other relevant material to industry, apparently with the notion that he would become an industrialist. Along with all these practical, scientific courses, Neville also enjoyed studying the philosophical works of Aldous Huxley.

After he finished his degree, Chamberlain was given a new task by his father: he was going to the Bahamas. Joseph had heavily invested in business ventures in Argentina, but as economic conditions in Argentina worsened, he saw his fortunes diminish. To recover from the financial setbacks caused by these losses, Joseph decided to direct Neville to a new project: managing a sisal plantation on the island of Andros.

Sisal is a kind of hemp used for various products such as rope and twine. Unfortunately, the plantation faced insurmountable problems. The soil on Andros proved unsuitable, and the sisal fibers produced were of poor quality, making the crop unviable for commercial success. Despite significant effort and investment—Joseph Chamberlain had sunk £50,000 into the project, a massive sum at the time—it became clear that the plantation would never yield a profitable return. In the end, Neville was bounced back to Britain after seven years of fruitless labor.

Upon his homecoming, Chamberlain went into business for himself. The largesse of his family helped him to acquire a metal ship berth manufacturer called Hoskins & Company. This outfit was a leader in the industry and even held a special patent for folding berths, which back in those days was a crucial component of passenger ships that transported large numbers of people. Neville worked as the company's director over the next 17 years, and this time around, he was able to oversee what was indeed a successful company. It was so successful, in fact, that in the coming years, Neville Chamberlain would come to be known as one of the leading industrialists in Britain. During that time, he learned not only how to take advantage of a winning industry but also how to make himself actively involved in every aspect of the process. It's said that he was a very proactive manager who would listen to the lowliest of line workers as readily as he would listen to a top engineer.

Chamberlain was able to regain his self-confidence through this enterprise, and he didn't take it lightly. Hoskins was his baby, and he was determined to nurture it as much as possible. In the process, he managed to kickstart several initiatives designed to benefit his employees, which were quite progressive for the time. Some of the causes that Chamberlain championed for his workers were concepts such as workman's compensation should an employee become injured, as well as special bonuses and even a guaranteed pension plan.

It was actually this same concern for the welfare of his employees that first opened the door for him to become more involved in public service. He became involved with the local Chamber of Commerce, served as a magistrate, and played a role in all of the latest over at Birmingham University. He also served on the board of Birmingham's General Hospital. Yes, it was his experience helping provide social services for his employees that would ultimately lead him to provide those same kinds of benefits to the British public.

Chapter Two

Chamberlain during World War I

"I was intended by nature to get through a lot of money. I should never be satisfied with a cottage, and having chucked away a competence . . . I am going to toil and moil till I grub it back again."

—Neville Chamberlain

Neville Chamberlain was quite busy with his civic life all throughout his thirties. In fact, he was so busy he may have neglected his personal life. The next thing he knew, he had turned 40 and was still a bachelor. In 1910, however, he quite unexpectedly met a lovely young lady by the name of Anne de Vere Cole, with whom he promptly fell in love. By all accounts, these two were a case of opposites attracting—Anne was every bit as emotional, social, and spontaneous as Neville was serious, logical, and cautious.

In January 1911, Neville and Anne were wed. Even though they were so different, Anne would have a huge impact on Neville's life. She encouraged him to delve deeper into politics and stood by his side every step of the way. She quickly became his closest companion, biggest supporter, and a trusted partner in everything he did. Shortly after their wedding, the couple moved over to the pleasant neighborhood of Westbourne. It was here that Neville and Anne would raise a family. Their daughter Dorothy was born on December 25, 1911, and their son Francis was born on January 23, 1914.

It's been said that becoming a father truly revitalized Chamberlain. He had previously looked toward the future with dread, as he did not want to grow old without a family. Most of his peers, after all, had already laid the groundwork of their family foundations many years ago. Neville likely thought that, for him, that ship had sailed. But thanks to Anne, he was able to show the world that it was better late than never. So it was that this man, who was already well into middle age, was able to finally have two little ones at home who would look up to him and call him dad.

In November of 1911, in the meantime, Chamberlain ran as a Liberal Unionist candidate for a seat on the city council to represent his old stomping grounds of Birmingham. He was successful in this bid, and from there, he steadily rose up the ranks, eventually being made chairman of the Town Planning Committee. Here, he ran things like he did in one of his factories. Just as he sought to enrich the lives of his employees, he tried to look after the general welfare of Birmingham's residents.

One of the great highlights of these efforts was the establishment of the Birmingham Municipal Bank, or BMB for short. This bank was operated solely by local residents, even though its very existence was opposed by the joint-stock banks of the day. Neville Chamberlain was a firm believer in bringing power back to the people, and it was through initiatives such as these that he sought to do that. These efforts, however, were somewhat diminished or even put on hold with the outbreak of World War I in the summer of 1914.

At age 45, Chamberlain was too old to be sent to fight in the war. Instead, his brother Austen recommended that he seek the new post of director-general of national service. He got the job in late 1916, but he had tendered his resignation by the summer of 1917. It seems that Chamberlain just didn't feel cut out for the job.

His main task was to organize conscription and recruit volunteers for various projects in need of serious manpower during wartime. No matter how hard he tried though, he was consistently unable to meet his quotas. He also felt that he had rubbed the then-prime minister, David Lloyd George, the wrong way, making his life altogether difficult. Although Chamberlain was disappointed at this dead end, he didn't let it discourage him. He knew that if he picked himself up from this little pitfall, he would soon be on to even better things.

It was on the heels of his resignation, in fact, that Neville Chamberlain decided to throw his hat in the ring for Parliament, running as a Unionist candidate for a seat in the House of Commons. He came out on top in this contest, receiving around two-thirds of the vote. Neville Chamberlain was 49 years of age when he became a member of Parliament and was put in charge of the Unhealthy Areas Committee. It might sound like a rather odd name, but this committee's primary focus was on the improvement of the decidedly unhealthy conditions that had been created as a consequence of the growing slums in cities such as London, Birmingham, Liverpool, Cardiff, and Leeds.

The war, meanwhile, would hit close to home for Neville when a cousin of his—Norman Chamberlain—became missing in action in France. He was later reported dead. It's been said that it was the loss of his beloved cousin that instilled in Neville Chamberlain a long lingering dislike of war—not just a dislike, but rather, an all-consuming motivation to try and avoid armed conflict at all costs. It was, of course, this same passion for peace and loathing of war that would be put to the test in his later years.

Chapter Three

In the Face of Economic and Political Instability

"My career is broken. How can a man of nearly 50, entering the House with this stigma upon him hope to achieve anything? The fate I foresee is that after messing about for a year or two I shall find myself making no progress. . . . But I can't be satisfied with a purely selfish attention to business for the rest of my life."

—Neville Chamberlain

After the war came to a close, Chamberlain focused on local issues like rent control and canals and waterways. While he gradually got used to life in Parliament, he wasn't too interested in the social side that often helped advance political careers. He even turned down a junior government role in 1920 because he didn't get along with Prime Minister Lloyd George.

Things then took a major turn in 1922 when Lloyd George's coalition government fell apart, and Bonar Law became prime minister. Chamberlain had been away in North America when the Conservatives voted to leave the coalition, but the political shake-up worked in his favor. He was quickly promoted to postmaster-general and later to minister of health, although this caused a lot of tension with his brother Austen, who had stayed loyal to Lloyd George.

When Bonar Law resigned in 1923 due to illness, Stanley Baldwin took over and made Chamberlain chancellor of the exchequer, despite his short time in Parliament. Neville Chamberlain now had the second-highest position in the British government. It was an incredibly fast rise, especially for someone who got into politics relatively late in life. However, he was soon delivered a political setback after the election of 1923 saw his party booted out of Parliament.

The loss gave rise to the Labour Party gaining control and establishing Ramsay MacDonald as prime minister. This state of affairs didn't last long, however, and after

MacDonald's government fell apart after just a few months, the British were back at the polls voting once again. This time around, Neville Chamberlain was able to best his Labour opponent and regain his seat. Interestingly, his opponent, a Londoner by the name of Oswald Mosley, would go down in infamy for founding the British Union of Fascists and supporting Hitler in the lead-up to World War II.

That same year of 1923 saw increasing tensions between Germany and France. Ever since Germany came out on the losing end of the First World War, France had been attempting to exact hefty reparation payments. It was when a cash-strapped Germany repeatedly defaulted on these payments that France sent in the troops. Soon, French troops occupied Germany's rich industrial region of Ruhr. The goal was to extract reparations in the form of goods like coal and steel. Yet no matter how many troops France sent, Germany proved simply unable to pay up.

The Inter-Allied Reparation Commission, which had been established after World War I to oversee reparations payments, struggled to manage the crisis. It was this dilemma that led the chairman of the commission, a prominent American banker by the name of Charles G. Dawes, to formulate a new plan. A special conference was held from July to August of that year, which resulted in the Germans agreeing to restart a reduced variation of reparation payments in exchange for a US loan. It was clear to many that this "rob Peter to pay Paul" arrangement—borrowing from the US to pay France—was not a sustainable solution. But at the time, it was viewed as a step away from hostility and a step toward mutual agreement.

The so-called Locarno Treaties, which were ratified in the following year of 1925, were viewed in the same light. These treaties called for cooperation and aimed to guarantee the borders between Germany, France, and Belgium, with Britain and Italy acting as guarantors. These agreements were intended to reduce tensions by ensuring that Germany would not challenge its western borders through force. This move toward an international collective security among these nations was yet another effort to bring about mutual trust in the hopes that future hostility could be avoided.

Further cementing this supposed goal was Germany's admittance into that international forerunner of the United Nations—the League of Nations. These steps toward collective peace were seemingly affirmed once again in 1928 with the forging of the so-called Kellogg-Briand

Pact. The main idea was that the countries who signed it agreed to settle conflicts peacefully instead of going to war. It was seen as a step toward lasting peace after the devastation of World War I, and eventually, 62 nations, including Germany, signed the pact.

However, all these efforts to bring the world together would come to a crashing halt due to the Wall Street Crash of 1929, which led to a global depression. As much as the great powers were trying to make nations interconnected, it was the very interconnected nature of the nations that led to the stock market crash of one of these nations to affect so many others. In particular, it was right after the US stock market crash that American loan money not just to Germany but to other European countries struggling to claw their way out from the rubble of World War I dried up.

Soon, Germany in particular found itself locked into a state of hyperinflation, with high unemployment rates and no immediate solution in sight. Rather than wanting to cooperate, there was an increasing lean toward a totalitarian government and the yearning for a political messiah who could save Germany from its economic downfall. That man, many believed, was Adolf Hitler.

Back in Britain, in the meantime, Neville Chamberlain was put back into the role of chancellor of the exchequer. In this capacity, he introduced important trade legislation, such as tariffs and import duties that were imposed on a variety of goods. Chamberlain also presented his first official budget in the spring of 1932, which included a significant reduction in the interest rate on Britain's own debt from the previous war—from 5% to 3.5%. This move effectively halved the portion of the budget allocated to wartime interest payments, easing the financial burden.

Chamberlain was also responsible for creating the Unemployed Assistance Board (UAB) through the Unemployment Act of 1934. His goal was to focus on the well-being of those out of work; he believed it was important to provide not just financial support but also meaningful activities to give people purpose during these difficult years of the Great Depression. On the defense front, Chamberlain initially cut military spending, but by 1935, with the rise of Nazi Germany, he realized the urgent need for rearmament. He especially pushed for strengthening the Royal Air Force, understanding that the English Channel alone wouldn't protect Britain from invasion with the growing threat of air power.

It took a lot of back-slapping and political wrangling to do all of this, but Neville Chamberlain proved that he was up for the task. It was a political crisis of a whole other kind, however, that would see Chamberlain promoted from the office of chancellor of the exchequer to that of prime minister itself.

Chapter Four

Becoming Prime Minister

"I should never have been P.M. if I hadn't had Annie to help me. It isn't only that she charms everyone into good humor and makes them think that a man can't be so bad who had a wife like that. She has undoubtedly made countless friends and supporters. And she has kept many who might have left me if I had been alone—but who are devoted to her."

—Neville Chamberlain

In 1936, Britain faced a crisis. It was largely a manufactured crisis, considering the fact that much of what was viewed as scandalous back in those days would hardly even register in the world of today. In brief, the then-king of the United Kingdom—Edward VIII—had decided to marry a divorced woman from America, Wallis Simpson. Wallis had been previously married to an American business mogul named Ernest Simpson. Today, such a thing might generate some interest from the tabloids, but it hardly would have called for the king's ouster. Yet back in the 1930s, it was indeed considered improper enough to generate immediate calls for Edward VIII to step down. It was simply considered beneath his station to marry a divorcee in such a fashion. His successor, George VI, was coronated shortly thereafter.

The prime minister, Stanley Baldwin, also stepped down at this time, and in 1937, the new king appointed Neville Chamberlain to replace him. Among his first official acts as prime minister, Chamberlain instructed his legislating ministers to immediately set in order and outline their legislative agenda of the administration. He was 68 years old at the time and had already lived a long and eventful life. Upon his appointment in 1937, Neville was more or less viewed as a respectful placeholder who would keep the seat warm until another general election could be held to make way for a new prime minister. As such, he fully expected his tenure as prime minister to be a brief one.

However, it soon became clear that this was simply not going to be the case. Chamberlain would remain as prime minister. The road ahead wouldn't be easy for him as the world became increasingly full of conflict and war. Japan had been fighting a bloody war against the Chinese since the early 1930s, Spain was locked in a brutal civil war, and the Italians had invaded Ethiopia in 1935. Germany, although not at this time as actively engaged in combat as these belligerents, was signaling that German aggression would be next.

Germany had since cozied up close to the fascist governments of Italy and Japan by way of the Rome-Berlin Axis as well as the Anti-Comintern Pact. Yes, despite the Allies' best efforts, Germany was not linking up with the democratic forces of governments such as Britain and France but was instead collaborating with the fascist regimes of Italy and Japan. The League of Nations, which had failed to prevent either Japan's aggression in China or Italy's aggression in Ethiopia, had proved to be relatively useless. No longer operating under any pretense of following its directives, Italy and Japan left the League, and Germany soon followed suit.

Rather than being influenced by the Allies, these belligerents seemed more apt to bully them into doing their bidding. Adolf Hitler, for one, seemed to relish seeing what concessions he could extract from his own saber-rattling. And it was Prime Minister Neville Chamberlain who was about to walk right into the trap of appeasement that had been set.

Chapter Five

The High Cost of Peace

"The condition of the Sudeten Germans is indescribable. It is sought to annihilate them as human beings. They are oppressed and scandalously treated in an intolerable fashion. The depriving of these people of their rights must come to an end. I have stated that the Reich would not tolerate any further oppression of these three and a half million Germans, and I would ask the statesmen of foreign countries to be convinced that this is no mere form of words."

—Adolf Hitler

In the spring of 1938, the Germans were once again making the British nervous by speaking openly of annexing Austria. Chamberlain had made it a major part of his strategy of deterrence in this particular field of German aggression to use Italy to pressure the Germans to back down. The Italians initially came out opposed to annexation, and the British thought that Italian Prime Minister Benito Mussolini was one of the few people that Hitler might actually listen to in this regard.

Chamberlain was making a deal with the devil, however, and was preparing himself for what would amount to, if not recognition, a de facto acceptance on Britain's part of Italy's unlawful occupation of Ethiopia. Once the occupation was in place, Chamberlain even advocated the removal of previous sanctions, stating that since the war was essentially over, sanctions would do nothing but inflame the situation further. This was a flawed argument on many levels. For one thing, the war wasn't over; the Ethiopian resistance had simply gone underground. Secondly, lifting sanctions on Italy without holding them accountable for their aggression sent a dangerous message: it signaled that successful territorial conquests, even those achieved through unlawful means, could be accepted without consequences. Such appeasement would only serve to embolden aggressor nations like Germany and Italy.

Chamberlain was greatly opposed by Foreign Secretary Anthony Eden for his views on these matters. Eden expressed his disgust with what he viewed as Chamberlain's quest for peace at practically "any cost." For Eden, such a delusional sense of peace was no peace at all. Eden was so incensed, in fact, that he resigned from office. This led Chamberlain to replace him with the appointment of Lord Halifax (Edward Wood).

Ultimately, neither Chamberlain, Halifax, nor even Mussolini could stop Hitler from annexing Austria, and the so-called *Anschluss* went forward in March 1938. Chamberlain stood up before Parliament and roundly condemned Germany's actions, but other than words, he did not offer up any relevant course of action against Germany. Instead, Chamberlain seemed willing to continue empty dialogue with Hitler and his cronies.

It wasn't long before the Germans were hungry for even more land. That May, Hitler began to saber-rattle about reclaiming the German-speaking section of Czechoslovakia, known as the Sudetenland. Interestingly, while Britain did not have any formal alliance with Czechoslovakia necessitating a use of force should another country compromise its territorial integrity, France did. Considering as much, the French had more skin in the game than the

British. Once push came to shove, however, the French were not so willing to fulfill previous commitments made to Czechoslovakia.

French Prime Minister Edouard Daladier met with Neville Chamberlain during this crisis, and they both basically agreed that it would be better to avoid war. Both leaders were also swayed by reports—some exaggerated—that ethnic Germans in the Sudetenland were being mistreated by the Czechoslovak government. From the Sudeten German point of view, even though they lived in territory that was part of Czechoslovakia, they were treated as suspicious foreigners from Germany. So, it seemed rather understandable that these spurned Germans might call for the lands that they inhabited to become a part of Germany proper.

The local champion of this cause was a Hitler lackey by the name of Konrad Henlein. Working in lockstep with the Nazis, Henlein had mobilized a substantial movement of Sudeten Germans who demanded the autonomy of the Sudetenland, though his real agenda was to bring the Sudetenland under German control. The Czechoslovakian President Eduard Benes was aghast at these developments, but with mounting pressure from both Britain and France, he was eventually forced to give up the Sudetenland.

Both Daladier and Chamberlain seemed to have come to the conclusion that if they obliged Hitler with this one last courtesy, they could have peace. They tricked themselves into believing that if they helped Hitler carve the Sudetenland from Czechoslovakia and make it part of Germany, they could avert a major crisis. Most other major players in the world, after all, could have cared less about an obscure little corner of Czechoslovakia. If having this small piece of the Czech pie could make the Germans happy and avert a world war, both the British and the French governments considered it well worth it.

With their minds already made up, Chamberlain and Daladier went off to Munich, Germany, to finalize discussions on this matter with Hitler himself. It was these talks that led to the infamous Munich Agreement, which basically handed Hitler the Sudetenland on a silver plate. Hitler did promise that he would not engage in any further aggression as part of the agreement, but could anyone trust him? In retrospect, we clearly know the answer to that question, but Neville Chamberlain didn't quite know what to make of Hitler at the time. He entered into the agreement with good faith and fully expected Hitler to live up to what he had agreed to.

Yet the whole pretense that Hitler had used to seize the Sudetenland was in light of the fact that the German minorities that lived there were being oppressed. Chamberlain rightly knew that there were other lands in Europe with significant German populations, such as the former German city of Danzig (which had since become part of Poland), where Hitler could try the same ploy. It was with this in mind that Chamberlain extracted a pledge from Hitler that he would make no further territorial demands. During the signing of the Munich Agreement, Hitler had more or less promised that all he wanted was the Sudetenland, and if this was allowed, there would be no further problems after that.

As much as Chamberlain is criticized for his appeasement today, the British public at the time was actually more apt to agree with Chamberlain and his efforts to preserve peace than they were not. The horrors of World War I were still fresh in the minds of many, and most people in Britain and beyond did indeed want to avoid war. Many felt that the First World War had been ignited all too easily and blamed the recklessness of world leaders eager for battle for the carnage that ensued. Yet, here was Chamberlain playing the polar opposite role.

Rather than making threats and stoking the fires of war, Neville Chamberlain was a statesman doing his all to avoid war. When he arrived back in London that fall, fresh from his talks with Hitler in Munich, he declared to have achieved "peace for our time." He told the crowds of people who greeted him that they could now rest assured that another world war had been averted and that they could all sleep peacefully and securely in their beds without any fear of air raid sirens waking them up in the middle of the night.

It wasn't until this peace was shattered with Hitler's subsequent invasion of Poland that everything changed. Was this the end result of Chamberlain's cooperation and compromise with Germany? Chamberlain had given the German government great concessions, only for the Germans to turn around and betray British interests. The British people were very quickly coming to understand the inherent limitations of a peace-at-any-cost policy. If Neville Chamberlain had purchased peace by way of his skilled diplomacy, the British public wanted their money back. They couldn't help but wonder just what this supposed peace that had been brokered would really mean in the long run.

Chapter Six

The March to War

"It is perfectly evident now that force is the only argument Germany understands and that 'collective security' cannot offer any prospect of preventing such events until it can show a visible force of overwhelming strength backed by the determination to use it. . . . Heaven knows I don't want to get back to alliances but if Germany continues to behave as she has done lately she may drive us to it."

—Neville Chamberlain

During his meeting in Munich, Chamberlain got Hitler to sign a pledge in the so-called Anglo-German Declaration, which promised that their respective nations would never engage in armed combat with each other again. Needless to say, these were some rather lofty goals for any two nation-states to commit to. Even so, Hitler signed the pledge regardless.

The notion that neither nation should come to blows with each other is, of course, open to the interpretation of what might necessitate blows. Hitler was likely fine with the idea of not striking Britain as long as the British allowed him a free hand in continental Europe. But no matter how much they desired peace, Britain could not just stand back and allow such things to happen. They couldn't watch as the Nazis gobbled up the territory of their neighbors. As such, it would ultimately be the British who were triggered to declare war on Germany in light of Germany's aggressive actions on the European continent.

The first real test of Britain's commitment to the pledge to never engage in armed combat against the Germans came on March 15, 1939, when Hitler—not satisfied with just the Sudetenland chunk of what had been Czechoslovakia—defied the previous protocols of the Munich Agreement and launched an invasion on the rest of Czechoslovakia. Making matters worse was the fact that Britain had its hands quite busy elsewhere at the time, with the Mandate of Palestine.

Today, the Palestinian-Israeli conflict is a frequent subject of headline news, but it is amazing how few know the actual history that led up to all this. The history itself is long and tortuously complicated, but nevertheless, it would be a great disservice to dive into Chamberlain's role as a steward of the British Mandate of Palestine without at least going into a little bit of the background involved. So, having that said, let's briefly discuss what led to this point.

Biblical Israel dates back a few thousand years, with the ancient kingdoms of Israel and Judah. However, the existence of an independent Jewish state came to an end when it was incorporated into the Roman Empire during the first century CE. The Romans ended up waging a brutal war against Israel, where they burned down their holy temple and kicked the Jews out of the land. The Romans then renamed their new prize Palaestina.

By the third century, the Roman Empire had become Christian, and Christians flocked to the land of Jesus, built churches, and did everything they could to Christianize the region. Then, in the seventh century, Islam came to prominence, and Islamic armies stormed into the region and seized control of Roman Palestine for themselves. Other than a brief interlude during the Middle Ages, when Christian Crusaders retook the Holy Land, Palestine would be under Muslim control for the next several centuries.

It wasn't until Britain defeated the Ottoman Empire (which sided with Germany) in World War I that the situation changed. Britain suddenly had control of the traditional lands of Israel/Palestine and, under the guise of the League of Nations, began to develop their so-called Mandate of Palestine. The British had a mandate to figure out the future of this troubled region but soon realized they had gotten a bit more than they had bargained for. By the time Chamberlain was prime minister, there were Jewish and Arab groups loudly clamoring for the right to have their own independent state carved out of the region.

Neville Chamberlain, as reasonable a fellow as he was, earnestly sought an equitable solution to make both parties happy. It was in this spirit that, in February of 1939, he invited delegates from as far away as Egypt and Iraq to come over to Britain for the so-called London Conference. The terms dictated here would have consequences from 1939 all the way to 1948, when Israel was officially declared a nation.

The conference itself, however, got off to a terribly rough start considering the fact that the Arab delegation and Jewish delegation refused to even sit in the same room together. Instead, they sat in separate rooms and forced intermediaries to have the tedious job of sending messages back and forth between them. Eventually, through this lengthy process, it was discovered—to hardly anyone's surprise—that the two parties were completely at odds with each other as it pertained to the future of Israel/Palestine.

The Arab delegation desired their own independent nation and refused even to entertain the idea of a Jewish state. They insisted on ending the mandate and replacing it with a new treaty that would further articulate their aims. They also wanted all Jewish immigration to the region to end immediately. The Jewish delegation, on the other hand, wanted to speed up immigration. A major reason behind this was the horrible persecution of Jews that had already begun in Europe at the hands of Nazi Germany. The Jewish delegation felt the need more than ever for the creation of a Jewish homeland that could receive this massive influx of refugees from what was becoming an increasingly hostile Europe.

Jews in Austria, Germany, Czechoslovakia, and even Poland were seeking refuge from the dangerous tides of antisemitism that were rising up all around them. The infamous episode of

Kristallnacht ("Night of Broken Glass"), which some view as a direct precursor to the Holocaust, had already occurred on November 9, 1938. During this appalling event, Nazi stormtroopers broke the windows, busted down the doors, set fires, and otherwise destroyed countless Jewish businesses and places of worship throughout Germany. During this melee, almost one hundred Jews lost their lives. For those who lived through this nightmare, it was certainly more than enough reason to seek refuge in a place like Mandatory Palestine.

It was with this in mind that the Jewish delegation insisted that the British should allow increased immigration for these Jewish refugees. Chamberlain knew that the Arab delegation wasn't about to go along with such plans. The so-called Arab Revolt had erupted in 1936 in a spate of anger over perceived inroads to a future Jewish state. The uprising was bloody and costly for the British; Neville Chamberlain, the man who sought peace, wasn't about to have more of that. Instead, he relied on an old tactic and decided to humor (one could even say appease) the Arab delegation instead. Instead of increasing Jewish immigration, Chamberlain let it be known that he planned to decrease it.

This move was not unsurprisingly highly criticized by the Jewish delegation, with future Israeli Prime Minister David Ben-Gurion remarking about how the lives of six million Jews were at stake. Sadly, this was approximately the same number of Jews that ended up dying in the Holocaust. With nowhere to go, millions of Jews ended up in death camps rather than Mandatory Palestine. We can criticize Neville Chamberlain today, safely removed several decades after the fact, but we must remember that he was a man with his hands full at the time, and he was desperately trying to put out fires—not (at least from his point of view) start new ones.

Shortly after the London Conference concluded, German forces were occupying the Czech capital of Prague. Back in Britain, Chamberlain had just given a glowing report on the situation in Europe and had painted a rosy picture of how his talks in Germany had worked out just fine. Hitler's unleashing of German troops on Prague mere days later made his words seem strikingly absurd.

Chapter Seven

A False Peace and a Phoney War

"I am myself a man of peace to the depths of my soul. Armed conflict between nations is a nightmare to me; but if I were convinced that any nation had made up its mind to dominate the world by fear of its force, I should feel that it must be resisted."

—Neville Chamberlain

In the aftermath of Hitler's latest aggression, Neville Chamberlain addressed Parliament, but his words didn't do much to assure anyone. It seemed that Hitler had taken Chamberlain by surprise, and now he was flailing at the wind in an attempt to get ahead of the problem. Chamberlain was caught off guard, and it was while he was still wringing his hands and trying to figure out what he should do about Prague that he learned of Hitler's ambitions for Poland.

In light of these developments, Neville Chamberlain held an emergency meeting of his cabinet on March 30, 1939, in which he declared full British support for Poland should the Polish nation's territorial integrity be threatened. The following day, on March 31, Chamberlain managed to get the French to follow suit. Chamberlain hoped that strong British and French backing of Poland would deter Hitler from going forward with his planned aggression against the Poles.

Interestingly, Chamberlain had also sought out an alliance with the Soviet Union, although he and many others still had their reservations due to the communist ideology of Joseph Stalin and his Soviets. In any case, the talks with the Russians ended up going nowhere, and Soviet Russia ended up turning to the Germans instead. Shocking the world, Germany and the Soviet Union signed a treaty of their own, a non-aggression pact. The most shocking part of this treaty was not fully disclosed to the public. The treaty contained a secret provision that called for the Russians to occupy the eastern part of Poland while the Germans invaded western Poland. Rather than protecting Poland, the Russians were much more inclined to take a piece of the pie for themselves.

As for Britain and France? Hitler didn't seem to think much of their threats of military action should he invade, and on the very eve of the invasion, he supposedly referred to the Western Allies as "small worms." The invasion of Poland would go forward, with German troops pouring into western Poland first thing in the early morning hours of September 1, 1939. Even then, the British dithered and held out hope that there might be a diplomatic solution. Germany was ordered to withdraw and given some time to do so. It was apparently hoped that the Germans could be browbeaten into doing an about-face. But of course, this was not at all what happened.

On the contrary, Hitler simply ignored Chamberlain's pleas, just as he had been ignoring his warnings and ultimatums over the past several years. Really, all Chamberlain's dithering did was make his own position seem weaker. In the midst of his seeming indecision, there were those among his opposition who openly wondered if Chamberlain was about to back down, cave, and do his own about-face and come out in acceptance of Hitler's invasion of Poland for the sake of peace.

However, Poland was a bridge too far even for Neville Chamberlain. He was not willing to appease Hitler any longer. And on the morning of September 3, Chamberlain gave an official address over the radio, indicating that Britain was now on a war footing with Nazi Germany. During the address, he explained how he had given the German government until 11 am to withdraw from Polish territory, but they did not do so. Chamberlain then indicated that his conscience was clear since he had done everything he could to avert conflict, but the Germans had left him no choice but to declare war.

But what kind of war was it? There were many who, in the early stages of this conflict, referred to it as a fake or "Phoney War." This was due to the fact that in the early stages of mobilization, not much action was actually taken against the Germans. This was something most keenly felt by the Poles themselves, who suddenly had Germans invading them from the west, followed by Soviet Russia's invasion from the east, with no apparent help in sight—at least at this early stage of the conflict. Instead of taking direct, immediate action, Chamberlain focused on rapidly bolstering Britain's military. He also initiated a blockade, which he hoped would damage Germany's economy and thereby slow down the German war machine.

The real threat to the German war effort, however, was any slowdown in precious resources such as oil or iron ore—the latter of which the Germans commonly purloined from Sweden. A key route for these supplies passed through Norway, which was neutral at the time. This led the British to consider a pre-emptive invasion of Norway in order to prevent the Germans from having access. In the end, the Germans beat the British to the punch since they too were planning the very same thing. First, in early April 1940, German forces took over Denmark. They then used Denmark as a launching pad into Norway. The British attempted to stop the Germans, but by April 26, they decided to cut their losses and make a hasty retreat.

Chamberlain suffered enormous political blowback from what was largely considered a botched withdrawal from the region. Of course, he wasn't solely responsible for these failures. There was plenty of blame to go around. The original plan had called for the British to quickly capture the Norwegian ports of Begen, Trondheim, and Narvik. For it to have been successful, the British needed to move swiftly. Chamberlain privately blamed the failure of doing so on British admirals who were plagued with an epidemic of indecision.

Nevertheless, Chamberlain was the public face of the administration, and it was Chamberlain who would have to shoulder most of the blame. The finger-pointing that ensued led to much political discourse and debate, and several cabinet meetings took place throughout the rest of April and into early May. There was indeed much to consider regarding the apparent military failures that were taking place. It was this wide-ranging political discourse that would ultimately lead to Neville Chamberlain tendering his resignation as prime minister.

Chapter Eight
Chamberlain Resigns

"The hour has now come when we are to be put to the test, as the innocent people of Holland, Belgium, and France are being tested already. And you and I must rally behind our new leader, and with our united strength, and with unshakable courage fight, and work until this wild beast, which has sprung out of his lair upon us, has been finally disarmed and overthrown."

—Neville Chamberlain

Chamberlain had initially sought to weaken the Germans by way of a blockade, similar to the sanctions that had been leveled at Italy in light of its invasion of Ethiopia. Chamberlain hoped the same sort of non-violent screws could be turned on the Germans to make them listen to reason. In particular, it was hoped that a blockade halting goods coming from Sweden through Norwegian ports and then on to Germany would impact the German supply of iron.

It was this very blockade that led the Germans to launch an invasion of Norway so as to seize control of Norwegian ports for themselves. As mentioned before, the British tried to fight back against the Germans but were ultimately forced into retreat. It seemed that this retreat was symbolic of all the other retreats, concessions, and appeasements made throughout the administration of British Prime Minister Neville Chamberlain. Even worse was when Chamberlain ignored intelligence reports, which suggested that the so-called Low Countries of Belgium, the Netherlands, and Luxembourg were going to be invaded by the Germans.

It was believed that the Germans would roll through the Low Countries in order to get around France's main defenses before launching a blistering attack on France itself. Chamberlain was briefed on as much, but he simply didn't want to believe it. Call it wishful thinking or pure and simple denial, Chamberlain just couldn't seem to entertain the possibility that such a thing would happen. Nevertheless, by early May, the Germans did just that. Neville Chamberlain had previously promised peace with honor, but after the humiliating retreat from Norway and the failure to stop further German aggression, the British public was becoming keenly aware that they were achieving neither. Even worse, this folly would soon be hitting close to home in light of German air raids on Britain.

Meanwhile, calls for Neville Chamberlain's ouster would only continue to grow. Those who knew him best felt bad for the rapid change in public opinion. Some even went so far as to liken him to Christ in the way crowds cheered for him one day and then called for him to be taken out the next. This perception was perhaps most famously expressed by British politician Collin Brooks. It was Brooks who pointed out that the same British public who had once hailed Chamberlain as a masterful politician were now calling for nothing short of his political crucifixion.

Not all of Chamberlain's political peers were quite so empathetic, of course, with the former Prime Minister David Lloyd George leading the charge against him. Chamberlain was roundly heckled by Lloyd George as having been duped by the Germans. The most painful charge was that Neville Chamberlain had failed in both keeping the peace and properly waging war.

At any rate, it was under all of this mounting pressure that on May 10, 1940, Neville Chamberlain officially resigned from the office of prime minister. Just prior to his resignation, he had conferred with King George, and both had decided that their preferred successor would be Lord Halifax. Unfortunately for them, Halifax was not interested. After it was clear that Halifax wouldn't take them up on the offer, their eyes fixed upon the prominent British firebrand Winston Churchill. Churchill would ultimately become the British face of World War II, eventually leading Britain along with the rest of the Allies to victory over the Germans.

In order to ensure a smooth transition of power, Chamberlain played a big role in getting things ready for Churchill behind the scenes—all of this leading right up to that fateful day when he officially tendered his resignation from office. The war moved along at a rapid clip after that. No longer a Phoney War, the Germans bulldozed through the Low Countries and right around France's main defenses. It was actually on the very day of Chamberlain's resignation that France itself was invaded by the Germans. Watching German tanks roll through Paris was not exactly how Neville Chamberlain wished to spend his retirement, but this was indeed the distressing backdrop of his first few moments out of office.

Chapter Nine

The Last Days of Neville Chamberlain

"All my world has tumbled to bits in a moment. The national peril has so swamped all personal feelings that no bitterness remains. Indeed, I used to say to Annie before the war came that if such a thing happened, I thought I should have to hand over to someone else, for I knew what agony of mind it would mean for me to give directions that would bring death and mutilation to so many."

—Neville Chamberlain

Shortly after Chamberlain's resignation, it's said that he just happened to run into a prominent American political official, who took the time to share his views on the then-rapidly unfolding situation on the European continent. This American official that Neville Chamberlain ran into was none other than Joseph P. Kennedy.

Joseph Kennedy, the famed father of American President John F. Kennedy, was at that time serving as the American ambassador to Britain. Kennedy apparently viewed the situation of the war as glumly as Chamberlain did and expressed to the now-former prime minister that he was unable to see how Britain could go on without its ally France. Chamberlain himself could not help but glumly agree with this estimation of events.

It was right before France collapsed entirely that British forces evacuated from France, fleeing out of the port of Dunkirk between May 26 and June 4. Even though the British were withdrawing, the withdrawal in itself was an incredible feat, which resulted in the successful evacuation of hundreds of thousands of British personnel. Although in retrospect Dunkirk would be viewed more favorably since it saved so many lives, it was viewed as yet another defeat at the time. Defeats that felt all too personal for Neville Chamberlain and only added to a long list of letdowns.

Neville Chamberlain's policy had proved feckless as it pertained to Austria, Czechoslovakia, and Poland. Chamberlain tried to save face and declared war on the Germans. He wanted to go on the offensive against the German war machine but struggled to find his footing. The British were forced to flee from the Germans in Norway and once again in France. It now seemed that the British were being defeated at every turn. Chamberlain resigned in the hopes that Churchill and others could turn the tide, but in the first days after his resignation, this did not seem to be the case. This series of letdowns and defeats took a personal toll on him.

It was shortly after the evacuation of Dunkirk that Chamberlain's health went into serious decline. He had been suffering from stomach pain for some time, but now it was considerably worse. One could argue that it was the stress of all of these debacles that exacerbated his condition. Even so, his resignation from office actually provided him with some sense of solace and relief. Perhaps demonstrating his true character, which utterly loathed conflict of any kind, Chamberlain couldn't help but be relieved that he was no longer responsible for making the life-and-death decisions of war.

Shortly before his death, he confided in his sister, Hilda, that he was glad that he wasn't going to be the one responsible for sending countless young men to kill and be killed. He even went so far as to speculate that even if the public was fully behind him and he wasn't pressured to resign as prime minister, he might have still resigned regardless. His own conscience simply couldn't countenance the tremendous shedding of blood that the coming war would inevitably bring.

At any rate, it was after he underwent an x-ray the following month that it was discovered that he was suffering from a cancerous growth in his bowels. His doctors realized how severe his condition was, and as the latest of a long line of calamities, Neville Chamberlain was informed that he did not have much longer to live.

Conclusion

On November 9, 1940, Neville Chamberlain breathed his last. He was 71 years old and perished in his sleep while resting at this rural estate located in Heckfield, Hampshire. A few days later, he was buried with full honors at Westminster Abbey on November 14. None other than Winston Churchill himself was among the pallbearers at his funeral.

Even after his death, the question would long remain: what kind of legacy did Neville Chamberlain leave behind? He might have had a rather rough last few months, both politically as well as physically, but even on his deathbed, he was determined to persevere. It's said that just a few days before he passed, he confided to those around him that he had made his peace with his decisions and regretted none of the choices he made.

Call him obstinate, call him stubborn, or just call him more far-sighted than most, for as much as he has been retroactively criticized for his appeasement of Germany, it can very well be argued that what Neville Chamberlain was actually doing during all of his long-winded talks with Germany, France, Italy, and the like was buying time. Germany had rapidly rearmed itself, and neither Britain nor France were quite ready to engage Germany on a full war footing. It could be argued, therefore, that Neville Chamberlain, while not buying a lasting peace, did buy some precious time—time in which Britain could prepare itself for war.

There are always going to be those who disagree with this argument, of course, and they likely have many good points to bolster their case. But nevertheless, in his final moments of reflection, Neville Chamberlain, for one, seems to have gone to his grave content with the role that he played. Having that said, his ultimate legacy and how the history books will ultimately view his efforts is still a matter of great debate.

Bibliography

Charmley, John (1989). *Chamberlain and the Lost Peace.*

Feiling, Keith (1946). *The Life of Neville Chamberlain.*

Macklin, Graham (2006). *Chamberlain.*

McDonough, Frank (1998). *Neville Chamberlain, Appeasement, and the British Road to War.*

Milton, Nicholas (2019). *Neville Chamberlain's Legacy: Hitler, Munich, and the Path to War.*